Living with Divorce

Activities to Help Children Cope with Difficult Situations

For Primary Grades

by
Elizabeth Garigan, M.Ed., C.A.C.
and
Michael Urbanski, M.Ed.

illustrated by Charles Ortenblad

Cover by Paul Manktelow

Copyright © Good Apple, 1991

ISBN No. 0-86653-595-0

Printing No. 9876543

Good Apple
1204 Buchanan St., Box 299
Carthage, IL 62321-0299

The purchase of this book entitles the buyer to duplicate the student activity pages for classroom use only. Any other use requires written permission from Good Apple.

All rights reserved. Printed in the United States of America.

Simon & Schuster Supplementary Education Group

Dedication

To our friends and families, especially our children Erika, Michael, Joseph, Tim, Timmy and Flynn.

In Appreciation

We would like to thank Sandy Webb for typing the manuscript for this book. We would also like to thank Mary Jane Cera, Judy Bisignano and Corinne Sanders for offering their suggestions with honesty and creativity. We especially thank Jim, Becky, Charlie and Ashley Duncan and the children of Kino Learning Center for posing for the illustrations for the story "My Mom and Dad Are Divorced."

Introduction

Adults may choose to play a significant role in assisting children with the divorce process. The most important thing adults can do is explain what is happening. Many times children create answers to unspoken questions that are much more frightening than the reality of the actual situation. Adults can also assist the child with clarifying his/her feelings throughout the process. The depth of the questions, answers and emotions will vary with the development of each child. Their questions about divorce will grow as they do. The following information is intended to assist children with the divorce process.

1. Children need to know what is happening to their families. They will usually create a much more frightening scenario without the actual facts.

2. Children need time to mourn over the loss of the old family structure.

3. Children need to know that they are not responsible for the divorce. Their behavior did not cause the marriage to dissolve.

4. Children need to know that both parents will be available to them. It might help to work with a calendar or practice phoning the parent not living at home.

5. Children need opportunities to work out their feelings and deal with their perceptions by talking, dramatic play, reading books or expressing themselves through the arts.

6. Children need reassurance from the important adults in their lives that these relationships will not change or will once again become stable over time.

7. Children need to feel confident that their questions will be answered honestly and openly. They need to know that adults will give them answers they can understand. Adults should take their cues from the children and answer only what they ask.

8. Children need to remain neutral. It is not fair to ask the child to take sides in a divorce.

9. Children need to realize and accept the fact that they cannot get their parents back together again. Many times children will have the hope and wish that their parents will reunite.

10. Children need to be spared the adult's judgments, anger and opinions of the ex-spouse. Children have a special relationship with that parent that should be encouraged and respected.

My Mom and Dad Are Divorced

Before the divorce, I lived with both my parents. We were a close family. We went places together and did fun things together.

We always went to Grandma's for vacation to play in the snow. One time we all made a snowman together. We all laughed at the snowman's funny old hat.

We always had fun on holidays. On Christmas we shared presents and ate good food. On Halloween we dressed up in costumes.

But sometimes at my house things were not very fun. My mom and dad would fight. They would get mad and yell very loud.

I hated it when my parents would fight. When they would yell at each other, I would get scared and hide.

I hid under my bed. Sometimes I would take my pillow with me. I tried not to listen, but they were very loud. I hoped my neighborhood friend Timmy could not hear them.

It seemed like they had fights every day. At first, I thought I did something wrong. I was afraid they were mad at me.

I thought about Mom and Dad a lot when I was at school. It was very hard to pretend that everything was okay.

I didn't want anyone at school to know my parents had big fights. I was scared that I would cry in front of my friends.

One day my dad and mom said they wanted to have a big talk with me. I was afraid they would yell a lot and be mad at me.

They were very calm. They told me they were getting a divorce. I started to cry. I wasn't sure what a divorce was, but it sounded very scary.

My dad held me on his lap. He said he loved me. My mom said she loved me, too.

My mom said the divorce was the end of their marriage, but it was not the end of their being my mom and dad.

Mom and Dad said their divorce was not my fault. They said they were just not happy living together, like when they first got married.

My dad said he was moving to an apartment. I would have my own bedroom, and I could bring my toys and pillow. If I wanted to, I could spend the night sometimes.

I was so angry at my parents for getting a divorce. I threw rocks and I got in trouble at school, but I didn't care. I was so mad!

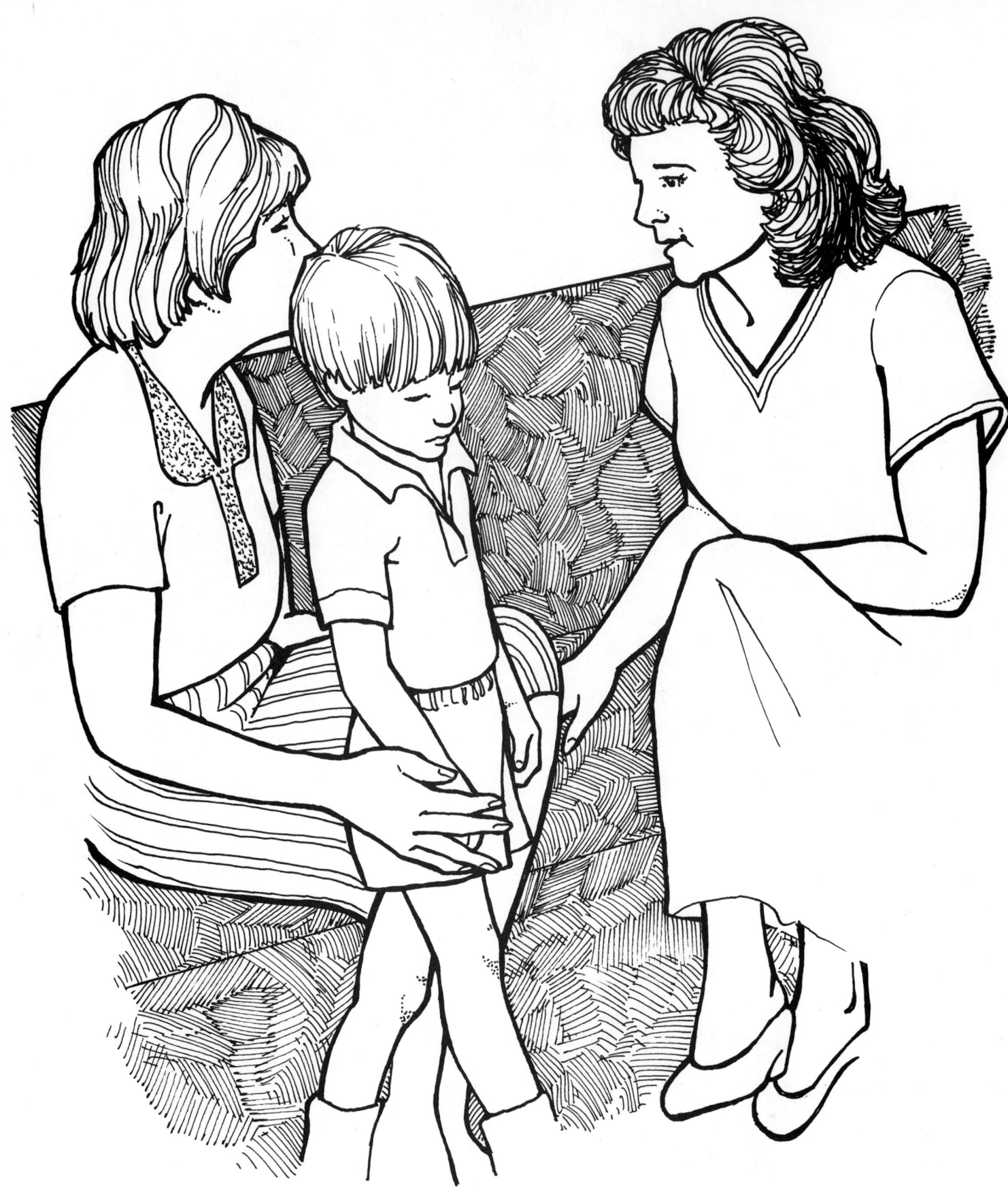

My mom talked to my teacher. Mom told her about the divorce. I just looked at the floor.

The next day in school we talked about divorce and feelings. I wasn't the only one; there were twelve kids in class whose parents had divorces, too!

We talked about our feelings. We talked about feeling angry. Lots of kids said the divorce made them mad.

We talked about feeling sad. Feeling sad is worse than feeling mad. Some kids felt very sad. Not me. I felt mad.

At home, my mom often feels sad. We give each other hugs to feel better.

My dad gets sad, too. One day I saw him crying. I told him that I often cry about the divorce, too. I guess I feel more sad than I thought I did. Anyway, I think I helped Dad feel better.

One day Mom and Dad went to court to see a judge. I'm glad I didn't have to go.

My friend Erin had to go to court with her mom and dad. She said it was very scary, but she felt important.

It has been awhile since the divorce. I'm not as afraid as I used to be. I don't throw rocks any more. I talk to my friend Timmy. His mom and dad got a divorce. Timmy understands.

My dad and I went to Grandma's this year, and we played in the snow.

This Halloween I dressed up with Mom, and we went to a party. She said we could do it every year.

I do special things with my parents. My mom and dad don't have fights any more. I like that part best of all.

I have met some new friends at my dad's apartment. It's different when I live with Dad, but I'm getting used to it.

It's even different living with Mom, but I'm getting used to it. Things are getting better and better.

I know my dad loves me. I know my mom loves me. They know I love them, too. I still belong to a family, even though my mom and dad are divorced.

Experiencing Loss

Life has many experiences of loss. The loss can be small, like a missed phone call. The loss can be big, like the death of a person you love.

Think about an "experience of loss" you have had. Write about your experience below.

_____

_____

_____

_____

_____

_____

_____

_____

_____

_____

_____

_____

You may want to discuss this experience with a person whom you love and trust.

Recognizing Feelings

In the spaces below, draw or find pictures and words that tell what each feeling means to you.

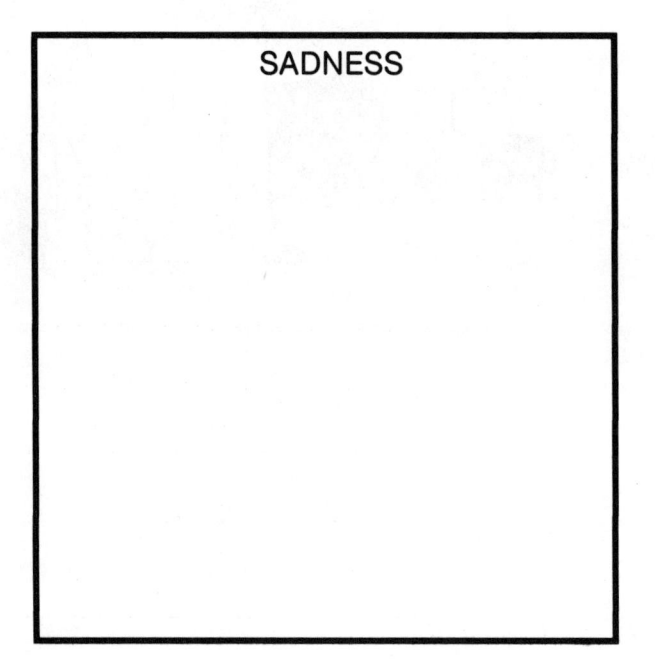

SADNESS

ANGER	HAPPINESS

Copyright © 1991, Good Apple 34 GA1314

Showing My Feelings

Sometimes, children are taught to hide their feelings. Have you ever been told, after getting hurt, that "big kids don't cry" or when you are upset, that "good children don't lose their tempers"?

In the spaces below, tell what you do when you have each feeling.

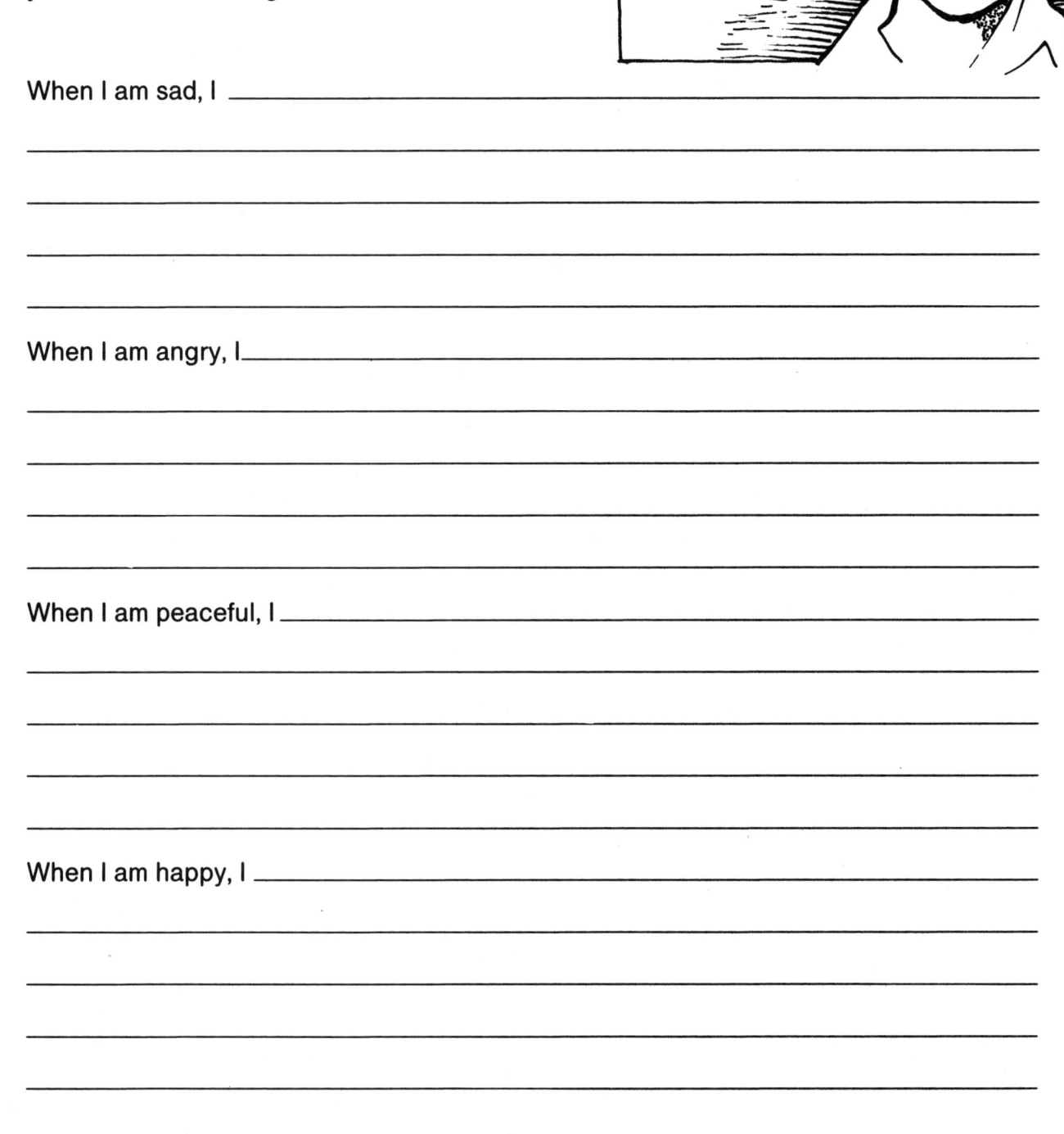

When I am sad, I _____
_____
_____
_____
_____

When I am angry, I _____
_____
_____
_____
_____

When I am peaceful, I _____
_____
_____
_____
_____

When I am happy, I _____
_____
_____
_____
_____

Changes in Nature

Nature teaches us about change. Day changes to night. Winter changes to spring. Every living thing has a birth, growth and death cycle.

Make drawings to show the changes in nature that might occur.

seedlings	flowers
rain clouds	sunshine

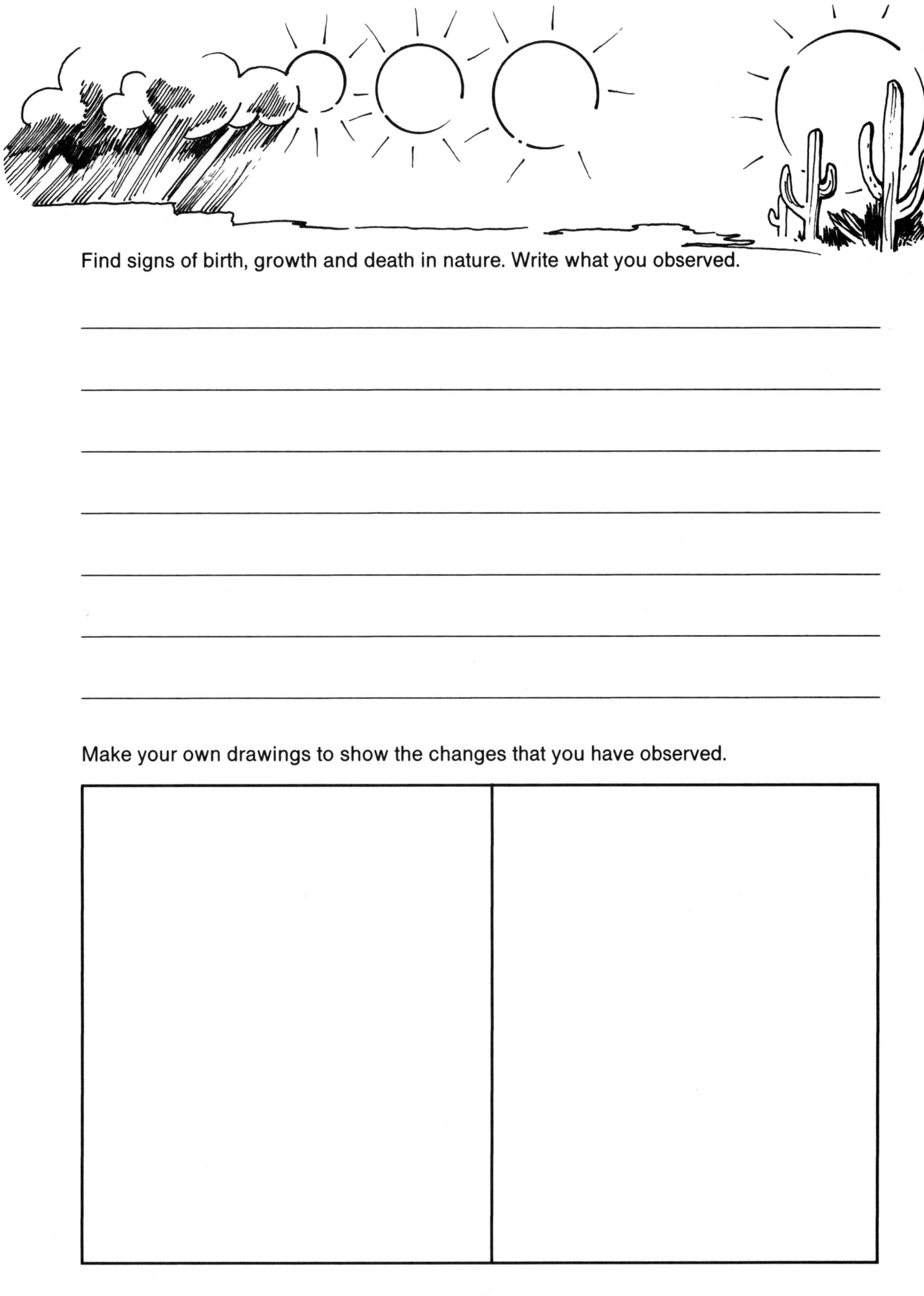

Find signs of birth, growth and death in nature. Write what you observed.

___

Make your own drawings to show the changes that you have observed.

Changes in Me

People, like other things in nature, have definite cycles of change.

Draw a picture of yourself at different stages of growth.

Tell about yourself at each stage.

Myself as a Baby
_____
_____
_____
_____
_____

Myself Today
_____
_____
_____
_____
_____

Myself as an Adult
_____
_____
_____
_____
_____

Changes in Friendships

Friendships, like marriages, also have definite cycles of change.

Write about a friendship you once had that has changed a great deal. Tell what was good about the friendship. Tell how or what the friendship changed.

_____

_____

_____

_____

_____

_____

_____

In the box above paste photos of you and your friend.

Quality Time with Mom

Find some time to spend with both of your parents. Remember it is the *quality of time*, not the *quantity of time*, that makes a difference.

Put an *X* to show how often you do the following activities.

ACTIVITY	OFTEN	SOMETIMES	NEVER
1. I talk to Mom and share my thoughts and feelings with her.			
2. I listen to Mom's thoughts and feelings.			
3. I tell Mom how much I love her.			
4. I write Mom notes and make special things for her.			
5. I spend quiet times with Mom without doing anything special.			
6. I would like to spend more time with my mom.			

Tell about the ways you spend quality time with your mom.

_____
_____
_____

Quality Time with Dad

Put an *X* to show how often you do the following activities.

ACTIVITY	OFTEN	SOMETIMES	NEVER
1. I talk to Dad and share my thoughts and feelings with him.			
2. I listen to Dad's thoughts and feelings.			
3. I tell Dad how much I love him.			
4. I write Dad notes and make special things for him.			
5. I spend quiet times with Dad without doing anything special.			
6. I would like to spend more time with my dad.			

Tell about the ways you spend quality time with your dad.

_____

_____

_____

_____

My Plan for Improvement

Happiness is often a choice you can make for yourself. However, you must plan for happiness and work toward it.

Tell what you do to make yourself and your life more whole and happy.

_____

_____

How often do you do this activity?

_____

With whom do you do it?

_____

Draw a picture or paste a photo of you doing this special activity in the space provided.

Set a personal goal to make this activity an important part of your life.

What's Next?

Draw, paint or find pictures and words from magazines that show your plans for the future.

Note to Teacher

The following activities are designed for use with students who are experiencing, or have experienced, the divorce of their parents. These activities may be used with individuals or in a small group setting. The teacher is encouraged to facilitate the use of this material—especially when a school counselor is unavailable. It is important that students have the opportunity to discuss these issues with an adult whom they respect and admire.

Taking a Survey

Now that you have read the story, "My Mom and Dad Are Divorced," you might have a better understanding of what *divorce* means.

In the space below, write your own definition of *divorce*. Ask five friends to write their definitions, too.

To me, *divorce* is _____
_____
_____
_____

My friends think *divorce* is

1. _____
_____
_____

2. _____
_____
_____

3. _____
_____
_____

4. _____
_____
_____

5. _____
_____
_____

Talk about these definitions of *divorce* with an adult whom you respect and trust.

My Feelings About Divorce

When your parents get divorced, you may have many different feelings.

Write *yes* in front of the feelings that you had when your parents divorced.

Write *no* in front of the feelings you did not have.

_____ I felt *guilty* because I thought I was the cause of the divorce.

_____ I felt *mad* because I thought it was unfair to have a divorce happen to my family.

_____ I felt *sad* because one of my parents was moving out of the house.

_____ I felt *scared* because my whole life might have to change.

_____ I felt *scared* because I was not sure if my parents still loved me.

Tell about another feeling you may have had.

I felt _____ because _____
_____
_____

Name someone with whom you could easily talk about your feelings.
_____

You may want to talk to this person about your feelings.

Expressing My Feelings

Feelings aren't good or bad. Just because you feel angry, it doesn't mean you are a bad person. But it is important to show your feelings in positive ways.

If you hurt yourself or others when you express your feelings, you might want to find ways of expressing your feelings in respectful ways.

Write a new sentence to change each negative sentence into a positive one.

Example: "I'm going to sit and pout until Mom asks me what's wrong."

"I'm going to be honest with Mom and tell her what's bothering me."

"I'm going to fight at school to get back at Mom and Dad for fighting at home."

_____
_____
_____

"When Dad (or Mom) takes me out, I'm going to make sure we don't have a good time."

_____
_____
_____

"I'm going to protect myself and not get close to anyone."

_____
_____
_____

Good Old Days

Tell about some of the things that your family liked to do before your parents were divorced.

_____
_____
_____
_____

In the box below draw a picture or paste a photo of one of these favorite activities.

Good New Days

Tell about some of the good things you like to do with just your mom, or just your dad, since their divorce.

_____
_____
_____
_____
_____

In the box below draw a picture or paste a photo of one of these favorite activities.

Writing My Thoughts

Sometimes during a divorce, words do not get heard. Mom and Dad may have been too upset to listen to you. You may have been too upset to listen to them. Here's a chance for you to express some very important thoughts and feelings.

Write separate letters to your parents. Tell them what you think and feel about the divorce. Don't hold back. You don't have to show your parents the letters unless you want to share the letters with them.

Dear Mom,

Writing My Thoughts

Dear Dad,

• IT'S NOT MY FAULT •

It's Not My Fault

Your parents are responsible for the divorce, not you.

In the space below make a poster with the words *It's not my fault*.

• IT'S NOT MY FAULT•

• IT'S NOT MY FAULT •

Then Whose Fault Is It?

Concerning the divorce, it is more important to accept the fact *that it is*, rather than *why it is*.

When you really think about it, does it matter? Why blame yourself, or one or both of your parents? Rather than think about what *could have been*, you might want to begin thinking about *what might be*.

However, DO NOT deny any feelings of resentment, hurt, anger or blame. Talk about what's bothering you with someone whom you love and trust.

Use the space below to express some of your feelings and frustrations.

_____
_____
_____
_____
_____
_____
_____
_____
_____
_____
_____
_____
_____
_____
_____
_____
_____

• IT'S NOT MY FAULT •

Looking on the Good Side

Your feelings of sadness and happiness are your own choice. You can look at new situations and new relationships in either positive or negative ways.

Change these negative statements to positive ones.

Example: New neighborhoods are strangers.
          New neighborhoods make new friends.

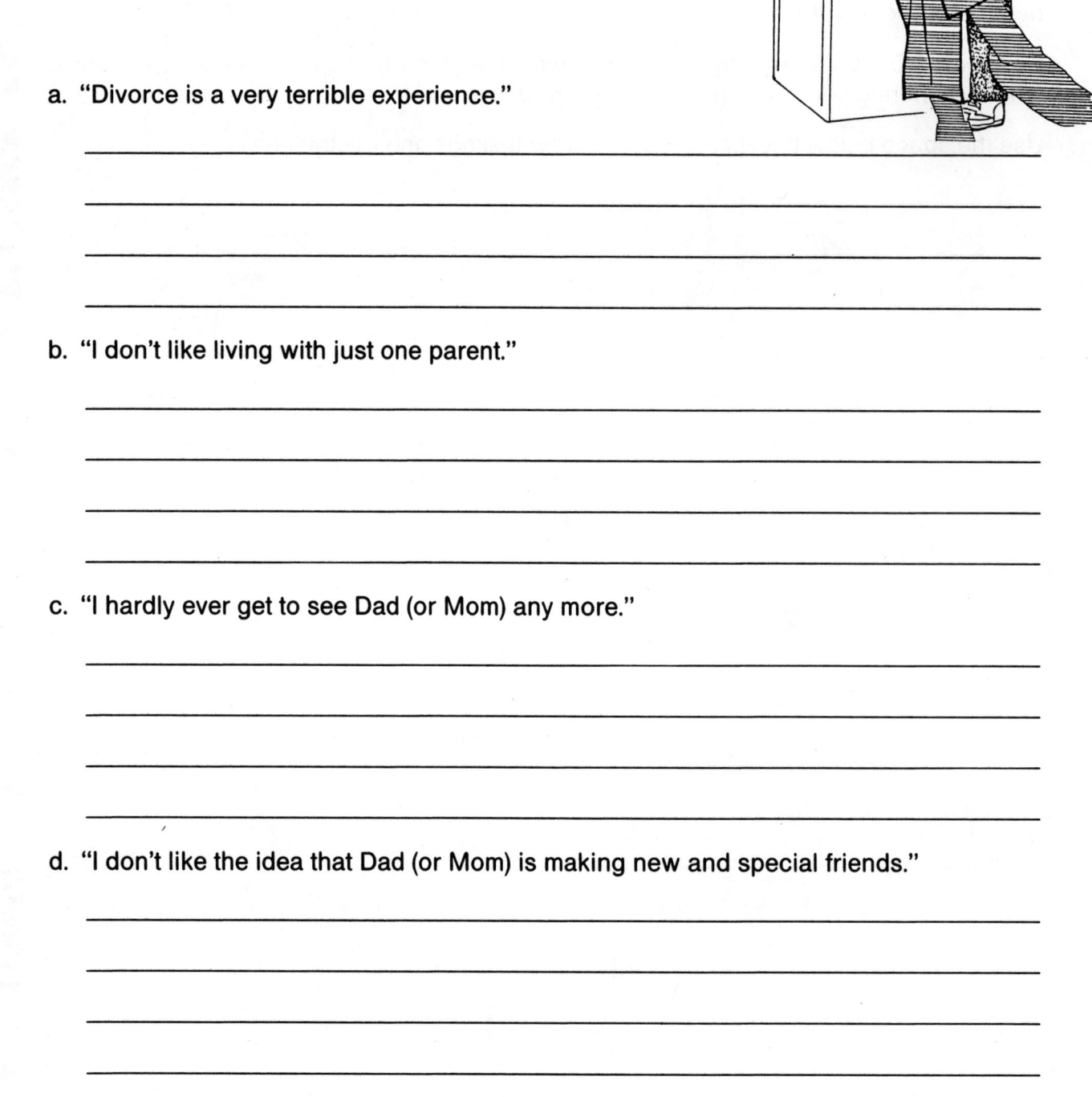

a. "Divorce is a very terrible experience."

___

b. "I don't like living with just one parent."

___

c. "I hardly ever get to see Dad (or Mom) any more."

___

d. "I don't like the idea that Dad (or Mom) is making new and special friends."

___

Making Things Better

List three things you like about your life since your parents' divorce.

1. _____
   _____
   _____

2. _____
   _____
   _____
   _____

3. _____
   _____
   _____

Tell about one thing you would like to change in your new family.

_____
_____
_____
_____
_____
_____

You might want to make a plan for change today.

_____
_____
_____
_____
_____
_____

Not to Worry

Sometimes you might be afraid when you think of not living with one of your parents. Make sure you know how to reach your parents. Find out when you can have time together.

Fill out this information page to use if you get worried about your mom.

NAME _____

ADDRESS _____

PHONE _____

Paste photo of Mom here.

WORK PHONE _____

WORK ADDRESS _____

DAYS I CAN VISIT _____

NIGHTS I CAN STAY OVER _____

THINGS WE CAN DO TOGETHER _____
_____
_____
_____
_____
_____
_____
_____
_____

You may want to put this information page near your telephone.

Fill out this information page to use if you get worried about your dad.

NAME _____

ADDRESS _____

PHONE _____

WORK PHONE _____

WORK ADDRESS _____

DAYS I CAN VISIT _____

NIGHTS I CAN STAY OVER _____

THINGS WE CAN DO TOGETHER _____

_____

_____

_____

_____

_____

_____

_____

_____

Paste photo of Dad here.

You may want to put this information page near your telephone.

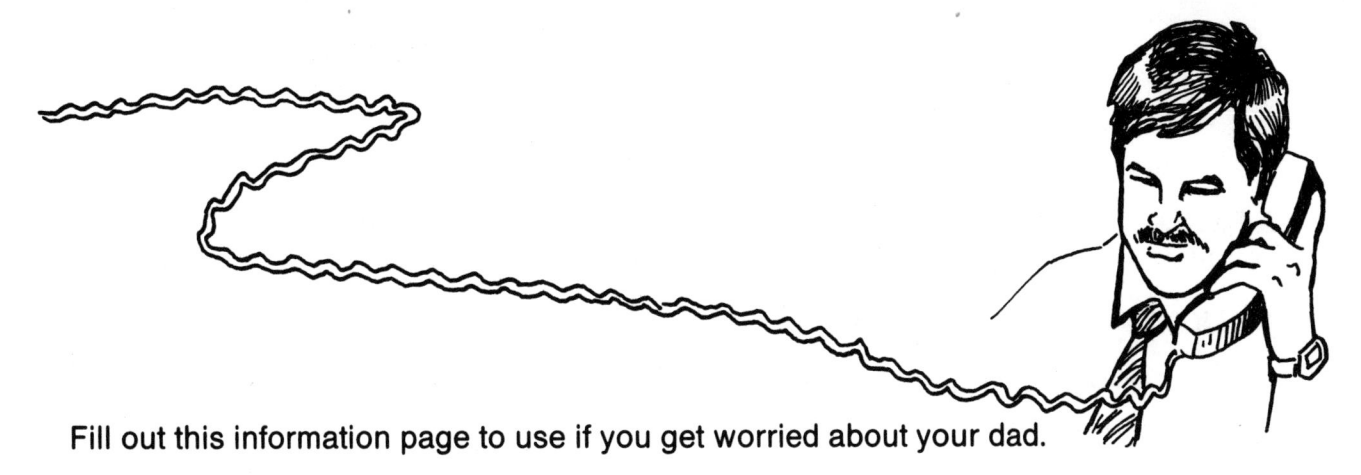

Vocabulary

A.F.D.C.—(Aid to Families with Dependent Children) Federal money used to help families with children

ALIMONY—Money paid to one spouse after the divorce for support

CHILD SUPPORT—The amount of money that is needed to pay for the necessary expenses in raising a child

CUSTODY—The parent with whom the child lives, who has the legal responsibility for the child/children

DECREE OF DISSOLUTION—The legal end of the marriage bond

DECREE OF DIVORCE—The legal dissolution of the marriage bond

DENIAL—The process of trying to believe nothing is wrong; ignoring facts

DEPRESSION—A feeling of deep sadness about the divorce.

EXTENDED FAMILY—Grandparents, aunts, uncles and cousins

GUILT—A very uncomfortable feeling of being responsible for the divorce

JOINT CUSTODY—The legal responsibility of raising the child/children equally shared by both parents

MEDIATION—The process in which problems between spouses are worked out with the help of a professional to come to an agreement

NO-FAULT DIVORCE—A divorce in which neither spouse is guilty of disobeying the marriage contract. The divorce is granted because the couple cannot live together.

NON-CUSTODIAL PARENT—The parent who is not responsible legally for the child

ORDER OF PROTECTION—A legal document, signed by a judge, prohibiting one spouse from bothering the other. The order is granted when there is physical or emotional abuse.

RECONCILIATION—The decision of a separated couple to live together as husband and wife

SEPARATION—The legal permission for a married couple not to live together

VISITATION RIGHT—A legal privilege given to a non-custodial parent to see his/her child/children on a regular basis

Bibliography

Anderson, Kihleif. *Divorced but Not Disastrous.* Prentice-Hall, 1982.
   Suggests ways to improve the ties between single parent mothers, divorced fathers and children.

Arnold, William V. *When Our Parents Divorce.* Philadelphia: The Westminster Press, 1980.
   The author is a pastoral counselor who deals specifically with concerns of older children and young adults regarding the divorce process. It helps young people to understand how their thoughts and feelings will affect not only their present actions but their future commitments.

Berger, Terry. *How Does It Feel When Your Parents Get Divorced?* New York: Julian Messner, 1977.
   This is a story about a twelve-year-old girl who faces the divorce of her parents with very strong emotions and reactions.

Blume, Judy. *It's Not the End of the World.* New York: Dell Publishing Company, Inc., 1979.
   The author presents a very interesting story of one person's divorce. Older elementary and junior high students really relate to the situation.

Booker, Deanna D. *Coping . . . When Your Family Falls Apart.* New York: Julian Messner, 1979.
   Author provides support and comfort, as well as some good coping strategy.

Brown, Lawrence Krasny. *Dinosaurs Divorce.* Boston: Little, Brown and Company, 1990.
   A practical guide for changing families.

Gardner, Richard A. *The Boys and Girls Book About Divorce.* New York: Bantam Books, 1971.
   This book was written for younger elementary-aged children. He discusses feelings experienced with divorce and provides support and encouragement.

Glass, Stuart M. *A Divorce Dictionary. A Book for You and Your Children.* Boston: Little, Brown and Company, 1980.
   A very understandable definition and discussion of terms relating to divorce.

Gripe, Maria. *The Night Daddy.* New York: Dell Publishing Company, Inc., 1971.
   This is a story about Julia's family and the reorganizing that took place as a result of the divorce.

Grollman, Earl. *Talking About Divorce.* Boston: Beacon Press, 1980.
   This is a useful resource for the younger child and may be a welcome aid to the parent explaining divorce.

Kolter, Neil. *Growing Up with Divorce.* New York: The Free Press, 1990.
   Describes specific causes of divorce. Illustrates specific problems and concerns for children of different ages.

Konigsburg, E.J. *George.* New York: Atheneum, 1970.
   This book is a story of a boy's very imaginative way of coping with the divorce of his parents.

Krementz, Jill. *How It Feels When Parents Divorce.* New York: Alfred A. Knopf Publishers, 1984.
> The author very sensitively photographs and provides interviews of children describing the divorces of their parents.

Le Shan, Eda. *What's Going to Happen to Me?* New York: Four Winds Press, 1978.
> The author deals with the entire process of divorce, from beginning dysfunction to stepfamilies.

Ricci, Isoline. *Mom's House, Dad's House.* New York: Macmillan Publishing Company, 1980.
> Describes how parents can make two homes for their children after divorce.

Richards, Arlene, and Irene Willis. *How to Get It Together When Your Parents Are Coming Apart.* New York: David McKay Co., 1976.
> The authors discuss marriage problems and feelings children have during and after the divorce.

Robson, Bonnie, M.D. *My Parents Are Divorced, Too.* New York: Everest House, 1980.
> Elizabeth, Michael, Jerry and Gordon, all teenagers, share their experiences and offer some very useful suggestions for coping with divorce.

Rofes, Eric (ed.). *The Kids' Book of Divorce.* New York: Vintage Books, 1982.
> This is an excellent book written by kids for kids!

Time-Life Video. Teenage Years. *Me and Dad's New Wife.*
> A great film about junior high school students who help one another deal with divorce and remarriage. Available at your local library.

United Artists—*Kramer vs. Kramer.*
> An award-winning movie about one family's divorce and separation, starring Dustin Hoffman and Meryl Streep.

White, Anne S. *Divorce.* New York: Franklin Watts, 1979.
> This book describes four older children's experiences with divorce and explains some legal procedures. Very easy to read.